Welcome!

Self Care is so important to your overall well-being. So many of us spend all our time taking care of others but neglect taking care of ourselves. As a result, we suffer emotionally and physically. By purchasing this journal, you have already made the commitment to take care of yourself and inevitably live a better life. *Congratulations!*

Included in this book are 12 weekly sections that help guide you to setting self care goals, hold yourself accountable in taking care of yourself with activity trackers, space to reflect on what makes you happy, learn to focus on the positive in your life while learning coping skills for the negative, and plenty of space to show gratitude.

At the end of each weekly section is space to journal and record whatever is on your mind as you journey through your discover of the benefits of self care.

Taking time out for yourself is an amazing gift you can give yourself every day. You deserve it!! I wish you the best as you travel through this journey of self discovery.

Positive Thinking

SELF CARE TO DO LIST:

- [ ] _____
- [ ] _____
- [ ] _____
- [ ] _____
- [ ] _____
- [ ] _____
- [ ] _____
- [ ] _____
- [ ] _____
- [ ] _____
- [ ] _____
- [ ] _____
- [ ] _____
- [ ] _____

PHYSICAL NEEDS

EMOTIONAL NEEDS

HOW I FEEL TODAY

I WANT TO WORK ON...

Affirmations

DAILY AFFIRMATIONS

Yes, You Can!

IDEAS & PROMPTS

I'm in charge of how I feel today, and I'm choosing to be happy.

I'm brave enough to climb any mountain.

I have the power to change my story.

I've decided that I'm good enough.

No one can make me feel inferior.

My strength is greater than my struggle.

I'll use my failures as a stepping stone.

It's not their job to like me. It's mine.

Success will be my driving force.

The only person who can defeat me, is me.

I dare to be different.

I do not need other people to be happy.

I deserve love, happiness and success.

I am loved and I am wanted.

I will not apologize for being myself.

Positive Thinking

POSITIVE THOUGHTS:
WRITE DOWN YOUR FAVORITE INSPIRATIONAL PHRASE

Do what makes you Happy

AFFIRMATION:

Self Care Techniques

MIND BODY

Good things take time

One Day at a Time

MONDAY'S MOOD

TUESDAY'S MOOD

WEDNESDAY'S MOOD

Good things take time

THURSDAY'S MOOD

One Day at a Time

FRIDAY'S MOOD

SATURDAY'S MOOD

SUNDAY'S MOOD

THOUGHTS & REFLECTIONS ABOUT THE PAST WEEK

Mood Meter

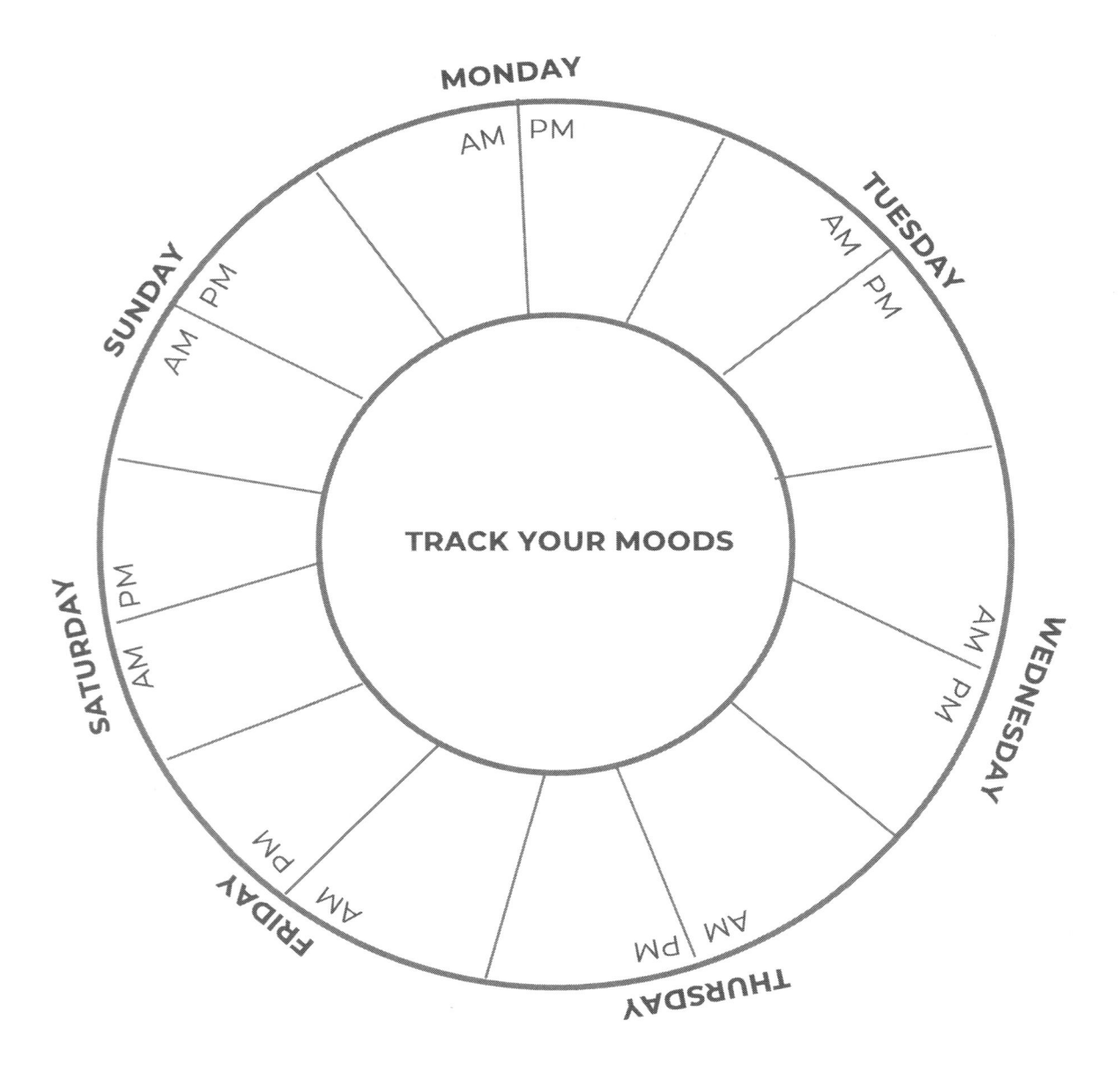

TRACK YOUR MOODS

- MONDAY — AM | PM
- TUESDAY — AM | PM
- WEDNESDAY — AM | PM
- THURSDAY — AM | PM
- FRIDAY — AM | PM
- SATURDAY — AM | PM
- SUNDAY — AM | PM

COLOR SCALE

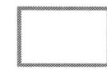

Self Care Checklist

GOALS	M	T	W	T	F	S	S
Got enough rest	○	○	○	○	○	○	○
Spent time outdoors	○	○	○	○	○	○	○
Drank enough water	○	○	○	○	○	○	○
Spent time doing Something that makes me happy.	○	○	○	○	○	○	○
Went for a walk or exercised.	○	○	○	○	○	○	○
Spent time with family	○	○	○	○	○	○	○
Meditated	○	○	○	○	○	○	○
Connected with friends	○	○	○	○	○	○	○
_____	○	○	○	○	○	○	○
_____	○	○	○	○	○	○	○
_____	○	○	○	○	○	○	○

Me Time

Write down the things that make you happy. Then, check the box every day that you spend time with that activity.

Do what makes you **Happy**

Self Reflection

SELF REFLECTION: WHAT MAKES YOU HAPPY?

Each failure brings you one step closer to success

AFFIRMATION:

Grateful Thoughts

THIS WEEK I AM GRATEFUL FOR

I AM BLESSED TO HAVE THESE PEOPLE IN MY LIFE

5 REASONS TO BE THANKFUL

1.
2.
3.
4.
5.

Self Care Log

HOW I CAN MINIMIZE THE NEGATIVITY IN MY LIFE

POSITIVE STEPS I CAN TAKE TO BE HAPPY

It Always Seems Impossible Until It's Done

DATE:

Positive Thinking

SELF CARE TO DO LIST:

- [ ] _____
- [ ] _____
- [ ] _____
- [ ] _____
- [ ] _____
- [ ] _____
- [ ] _____
- [ ] _____
- [ ] _____
- [ ] _____
- [ ] _____
- [ ] _____
- [ ] _____
- [ ] _____

PHYSICAL NEEDS

EMOTIONAL NEEDS

HOW I FEEL TODAY

I WANT TO WORK ON...

Affirmations

DAILY AFFIRMATIONS

IDEAS & PROMPTS

I'm in charge of how I feel today, and I'm choosing to be happy.

I'm brave enough to climb any mountain.

I have the power to change my story.

I've decided that I'm good enough.

No one can make me feel inferior.

My strength is greater than my struggle.

I'll use my failures as a stepping stone.

It's not their job to like me. It's mine.

Success will be my driving force.

The only person who can defeat me, is me.

I dare to be different.

I do not need other people to be happy.

I deserve love, happiness and success.

I am loved and I am wanted.

I will not apologize for being myself.

Yes, You Can!

Positive Thinking

POSITIVE THOUGHTS:
WRITE DOWN YOUR FAVORITE INSPIRATIONAL PHRASE

Do what makes you Happy

AFFIRMATION:

Self Care Techniques

MIND

_____
_____
_____
_____
_____
_____
_____
_____
_____
_____
_____

BODY

_____
_____
_____
_____
_____
_____
_____
_____
_____
_____
_____

Good things take time

One Day at a Time

MONDAY'S **MOOD**

TUESDAY'S **MOOD**

WEDNESDAY'S **MOOD**

Good things take time

THURSDAY'S **MOOD**

One Day at a Time

FRIDAY'S MOOD

SATURDAY'S MOOD

SUNDAY'S MOOD

THOUGHTS & REFLECTIONS ABOUT THE PAST WEEK

Mood Meter

MONDAY — AM | PM
TUESDAY — AM | PM
WEDNESDAY — AM | PM
THURSDAY — AM | PM
FRIDAY — AM | PM
SATURDAY — AM | PM
SUNDAY — AM | PM

TRACK YOUR MOODS

COLOR SCALE

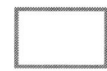

Self Care Checklist

GOALS	M	T	W	T	F	S	S
Got enough rest	○	○	○	○	○	○	○
Spent time outdoors	○	○	○	○	○	○	○
Drank enough water	○	○	○	○	○	○	○
Spent time doing Something that makes me happy.	○	○	○	○	○	○	○
Went for a walk or exercised.	○	○	○	○	○	○	○
Spent time with family	○	○	○	○	○	○	○
Meditated	○	○	○	○	○	○	○
Connected with friends	○	○	○	○	○	○	○
_____	○	○	○	○	○	○	○
_____	○	○	○	○	○	○	○
_____	○	○	○	○	○	○	○

Me Time

Write down the things that make you happy. Then, check the box every day that you spend time with that activity.

Do what makes you Happy

Self Reflection

SELF REFLECTION: WHAT MAKES YOU HAPPY?

Each failure brings you one step closer to success

AFFIRMATION:

Grateful Thoughts

THIS WEEK I AM GRATEFUL FOR

I AM BLESSED TO HAVE THESE PEOPLE IN MY LIFE

5 REASONS TO BE THANKFUL

1.
2.
3.
4.
5.

Self Care Log

HOW I CAN MINIMIZE THE NEGATIVITY IN MY LIFE

POSITIVE STEPS I CAN TAKE TO BE HAPPY

It Always Seems Impossible Until It's Done

DATE:

Positive Thinking

SELF CARE TO DO LIST:

- ☐ _____
- ☐ _____
- ☐ _____
- ☐ _____
- ☐ _____
- ☐ _____
- ☐ _____
- ☐ _____
- ☐ _____
- ☐ _____
- ☐ _____
- ☐ _____
- ☐ _____
- ☐ _____

PHYSICAL NEEDS

EMOTIONAL NEEDS

HOW I FEEL TODAY

I WANT TO WORK ON...

Affirmations

DAILY AFFIRMATIONS

Yes, You Can!

IDEAS & PROMPTS

I'm in charge of how I feel today, and I'm choosing to be happy.

I'm brave enough to climb any mountain.

I have the power to change my story.

I've decided that I'm good enough.

No one can make me feel inferior.

My strength is greater than my struggle.

I'll use my failures as a stepping stone.

It's not their job to like me. It's mine.

Success will be my driving force.

The only person who can defeat me, is me.

I dare to be different.

I do not need other people to be happy.

I deserve love, happiness and success.

I am loved and I am wanted.

I will not apologize for being myself.

Positive Thinking

POSITIVE THOUGHTS:
WRITE DOWN YOUR FAVORITE INSPIRATIONAL PHRASE

Do what makes you Happy

AFFIRMATION:

Self Care Techniques

MIND | BODY

Good things take time

One Day at a Time

MONDAY'S **MOOD**

TUESDAY'S **MOOD**

WEDNESDAY'S **MOOD**

Good things take time

THURSDAY'S **MOOD**

One Day at a Time

FRIDAY'S MOOD

SATURDAY'S MOOD

SUNDAY'S MOOD

THOUGHTS & REFLECTIONS ABOUT THE PAST WEEK

Mood Meter

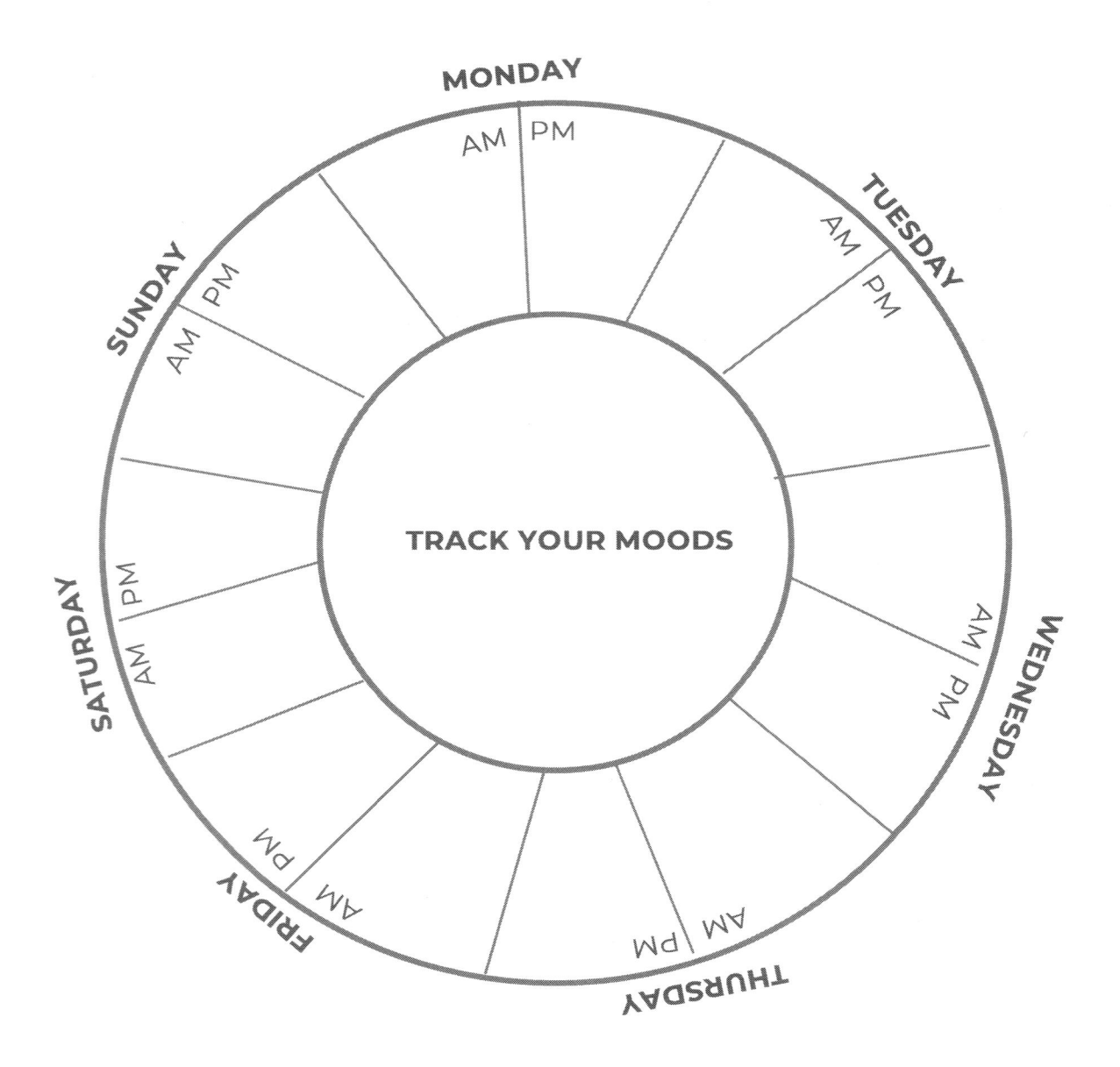

MONDAY
AM | PM

TUESDAY
AM | PM

WEDNESDAY
AM | PM

THURSDAY
AM | PM

FRIDAY
AM | PM

SATURDAY
AM | PM

SUNDAY
AM | PM

TRACK YOUR MOODS

COLOR SCALE

Self Care Checklist

GOALS	M	T	W	T	F	S	S
Got enough rest	○	○	○	○	○	○	○
Spent time outdoors	○	○	○	○	○	○	○
Drank enough water	○	○	○	○	○	○	○
Spent time doing Something that makes me happy.	○	○	○	○	○	○	○
Went for a walk or exercised.	○	○	○	○	○	○	○
Spent time with family	○	○	○	○	○	○	○
Meditated	○	○	○	○	○	○	○
Connected with friends	○	○	○	○	○	○	○
_____	○	○	○	○	○	○	○
_____	○	○	○	○	○	○	○
_____	○	○	○	○	○	○	○

Me Time

Write down the things that make you happy. Then, check the box every day that you spend time with that activity.

Do what makes you Happy

Self Reflection

SELF REFLECTION: WHAT MAKES YOU HAPPY?

Each failure brings you one step closer to success

AFFIRMATION:

Grateful Thoughts

THIS WEEK I AM GRATEFUL FOR

I AM BLESSED TO HAVE THESE PEOPLE IN MY LIFE

5 REASONS TO BE THANKFUL

1
2
3
4
5

Self Care Log

HOW I CAN **MINIMIZE THE NEGATIVITY** IN MY LIFE

POSITIVE STEPS I CAN TAKE TO BE HAPPY

It Always Seems Impossible Until It's Done

DATE:

Positive Thinking

SELF CARE TO DO LIST:

- [ ] _____
- [ ] _____
- [ ] _____
- [ ] _____
- [ ] _____
- [ ] _____
- [ ] _____
- [ ] _____
- [ ] _____
- [ ] _____
- [ ] _____
- [ ] _____
- [ ] _____
- [ ] _____
- [ ] _____

PHYSICAL NEEDS

EMOTIONAL NEEDS

HOW I FEEL TODAY

I WANT TO WORK ON...

Affirmations

DAILY AFFIRMATIONS

IDEAS & PROMPTS

I'm in charge of how I feel today, and I'm choosing to be happy.

I'm brave enough to climb any mountain.

I have the power to change my story.

I've decided that I'm good enough.

No one can make me feel inferior.

My strength is greater than my struggle.

I'll use my failures as a stepping stone.

It's not their job to like me. It's mine.

Success will be my driving force.

The only person who can defeat me, is me.

I dare to be different.

I do not need other people to be happy.

I deserve love, happiness and success.

I am loved and I am wanted.

I will not apologize for being myself.

Yes, You Can!

Positive Thinking

POSITIVE THOUGHTS:
WRITE DOWN YOUR FAVORITE INSPIRATIONAL PHRASE

Do what makes you Happy

AFFIRMATION:

Self Care Techniques

MIND

_____
_____
_____
_____
_____
_____
_____
_____
_____
_____

BODY

_____
_____
_____
_____
_____
_____
_____
_____
_____
_____

Good things take time

One Day at a Time

MONDAY'S MOOD

TUESDAY'S MOOD

WEDNESDAY'S MOOD

Good things take time

THURSDAY'S MOOD

One Day at a Time

FRIDAY'S MOOD

SATURDAY'S MOOD

SUNDAY'S MOOD

THOUGHTS & REFLECTIONS ABOUT THE PAST WEEK

Mood Meter

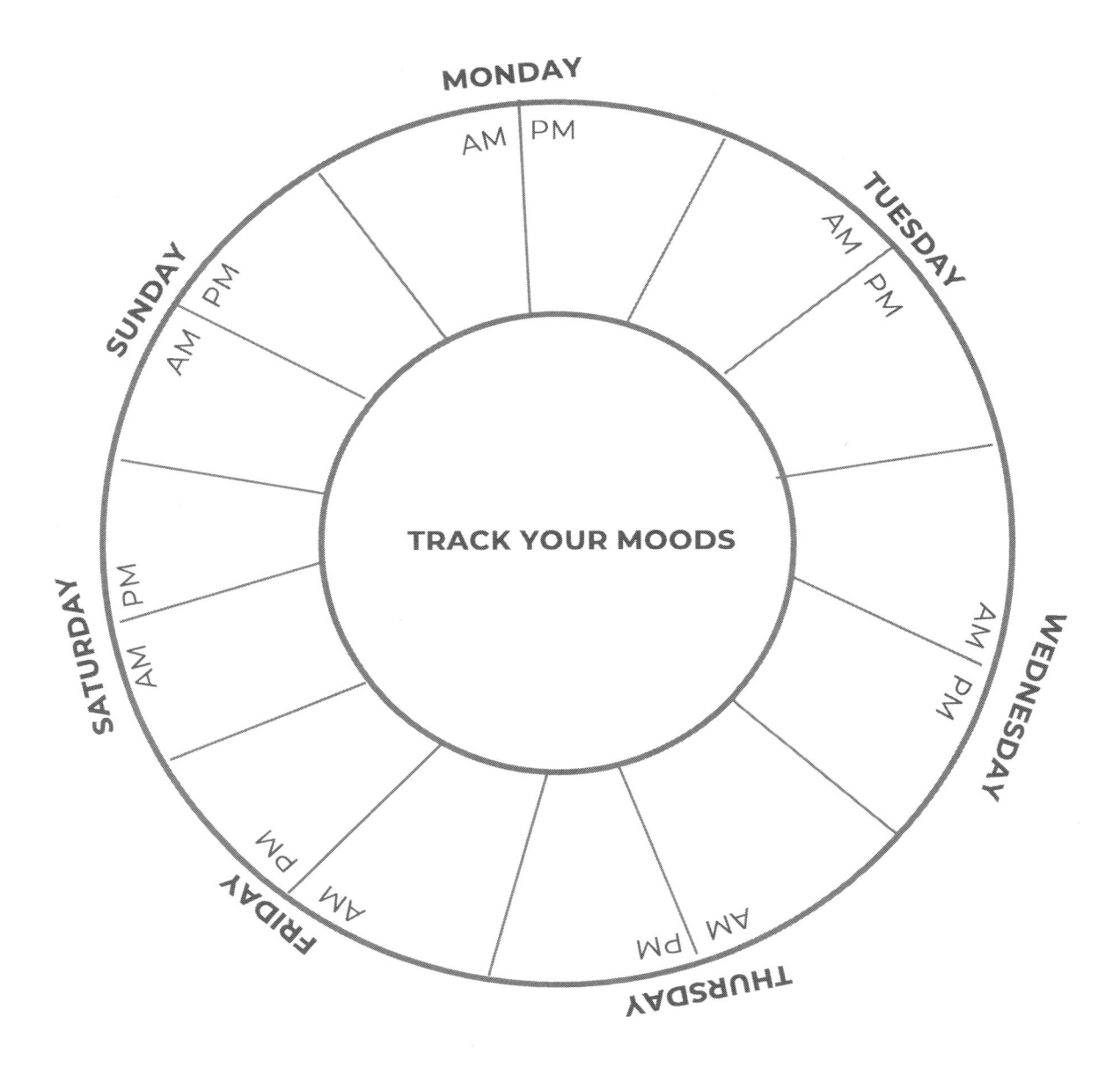

MONDAY | AM | PM
TUESDAY | AM | PM
WEDNESDAY | AM | PM
THURSDAY | AM | PM
FRIDAY | AM | PM
SATURDAY | AM | PM
SUNDAY | AM | PM

TRACK YOUR MOODS

COLOR SCALE

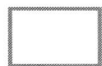

Self Care Checklist

GOALS	M	T	W	T	F	S	S
Got enough rest	○	○	○	○	○	○	○
Spent time outdoors	○	○	○	○	○	○	○
Drank enough water	○	○	○	○	○	○	○
Spent time doing Something that makes me happy.	○	○	○	○	○	○	○
Went for a walk or exercised.	○	○	○	○	○	○	○
Spent time with family	○	○	○	○	○	○	○
Meditated	○	○	○	○	○	○	○
Connected with friends	○	○	○	○	○	○	○
_____	○	○	○	○	○	○	○
_____	○	○	○	○	○	○	○
_____	○	○	○	○	○	○	○

Me Time

Write down the things that make you happy. Then, check the box every day that you spend time with that activity.

Do what makes you Happy

Self Reflection

SELF REFLECTION: WHAT MAKES YOU HAPPY?

Each failure brings you one step closer to success

AFFIRMATION:

Grateful Thoughts

THIS WEEK I AM GRATEFUL FOR

I AM BLESSED TO HAVE THESE PEOPLE IN MY LIFE

5 REASONS TO BE THANKFUL

1
2
3
4
5

Self Care Log

HOW I CAN **MINIMIZE THE NEGATIVITY** IN MY LIFE

POSITIVE STEPS I CAN TAKE TO BE HAPPY

It Always Seems Impossible Until It's Done

DATE:

Positive Thinking

SELF CARE TO DO LIST:

- [ ] _____
- [ ] _____
- [ ] _____
- [ ] _____
- [ ] _____
- [ ] _____
- [ ] _____
- [ ] _____
- [ ] _____
- [ ] _____
- [ ] _____
- [ ] _____
- [ ] _____
- [ ] _____

PHYSICAL NEEDS

EMOTIONAL NEEDS

HOW I FEEL TODAY

I WANT TO WORK ON...

Affirmations

DAILY AFFIRMATIONS

Yes, You Can!

IDEAS & PROMPTS

I'm in charge of how I feel today, and I'm choosing to be happy.

I'm brave enough to climb any mountain.

I have the power to change my story.

I've decided that I'm good enough.

No one can make me feel inferior.

My strength is greater than my struggle.

I'll use my failures as a stepping stone.

It's not their job to like me. It's mine.

Success will be my driving force.

The only person who can defeat me, is me.

I dare to be different.

I do not need other people to be happy.

I deserve love, happiness and success.

I am loved and I am wanted.

I will not apologize for being myself.

Positive Thinking

POSITIVE THOUGHTS:
WRITE DOWN YOUR FAVORITE INSPIRATIONAL PHRASE

Do what makes you Happy

AFFIRMATION:

Self Care Techniques

MIND

_____
_____
_____
_____
_____
_____
_____
_____
_____
_____

BODY

_____
_____
_____
_____
_____
_____
_____
_____
_____
_____

Good things take time

One Day at a Time

MONDAY'S MOOD

TUESDAY'S MOOD

WEDNESDAY'S MOOD

Good things take time

THURSDAY'S MOOD

One Day at a Time

FRIDAY'S MOOD

SATURDAY'S MOOD

SUNDAY'S MOOD

THOUGHTS & REFLECTIONS ABOUT THE PAST WEEK

Mood Meter

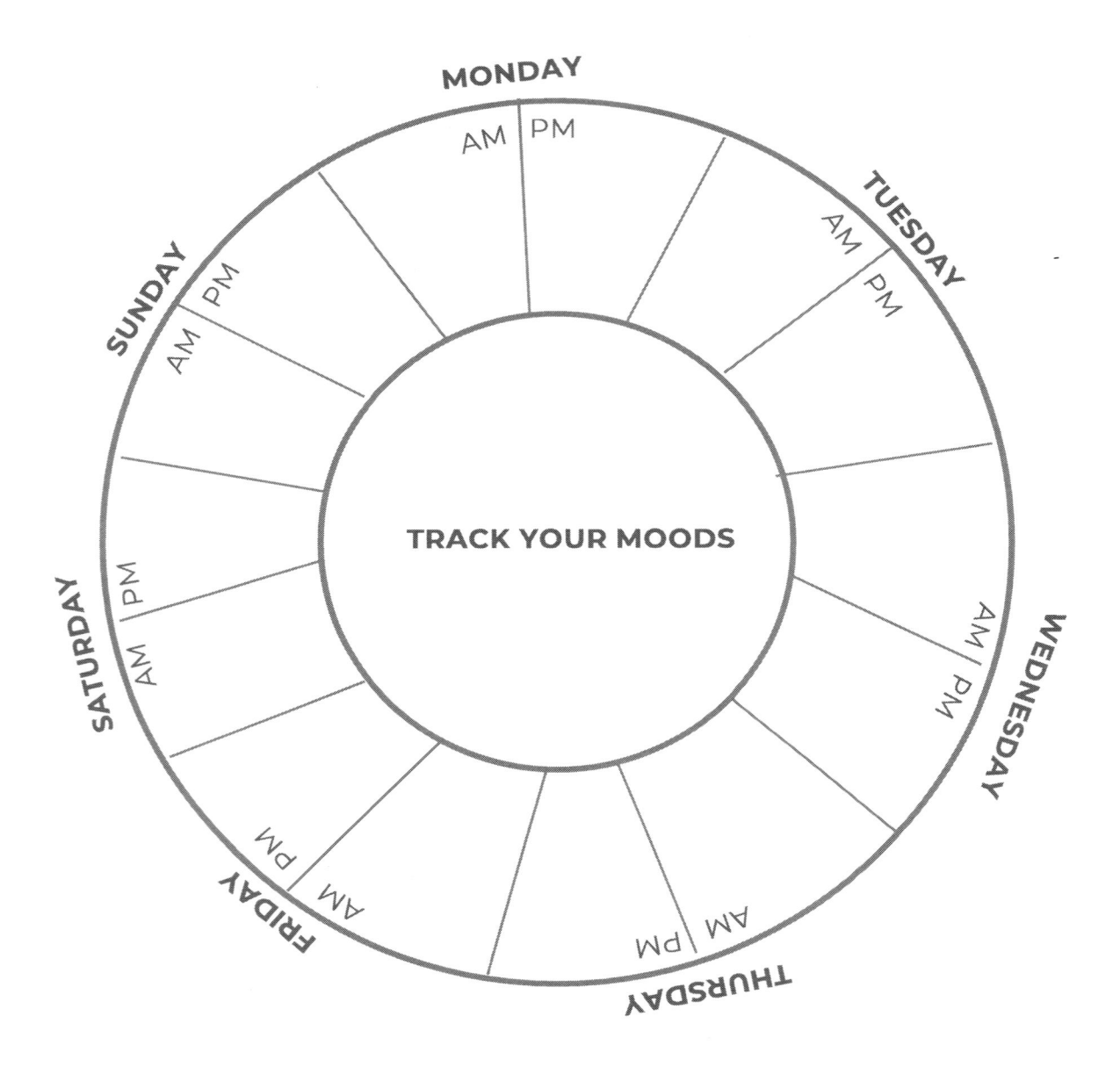

MONDAY
TUESDAY
WEDNESDAY
THURSDAY
FRIDAY
SATURDAY
SUNDAY

AM | PM

TRACK YOUR MOODS

COLOR SCALE

Self Care Checklist

GOALS	M	T	W	T	F	S	S
Got enough rest	○	○	○	○	○	○	○
Spent time outdoors	○	○	○	○	○	○	○
Drank enough water	○	○	○	○	○	○	○
Spent time doing Something that makes me happy.	○	○	○	○	○	○	○
Went for a walk or exercised.	○	○	○	○	○	○	○
Spent time with family	○	○	○	○	○	○	○
Meditated	○	○	○	○	○	○	○
Connected with friends	○	○	○	○	○	○	○
_____	○	○	○	○	○	○	○
_____	○	○	○	○	○	○	○
_____	○	○	○	○	○	○	○

Me Time

Write down the things that make you happy. Then, check the box every day that you spend time with that activity.

Do what makes you Happy

Self Reflection

SELF REFLECTION: WHAT MAKES YOU HAPPY?

Each failure brings you one step closer to success

AFFIRMATION:

Grateful Thoughts

THIS WEEK I AM GRATEFUL FOR

I AM BLESSED TO HAVE THESE PEOPLE IN MY LIFE

5 REASONS TO BE THANKFUL

1
2
3
4
5

Self Care Log

HOW I CAN MINIMIZE THE NEGATIVITY IN MY LIFE

POSITIVE STEPS I CAN TAKE TO BE HAPPY

It Always Seems Impossible Until It's Done

DATE:

Positive Thinking

SELF CARE TO DO LIST:

- [ ]
- [ ]
- [ ]
- [ ]
- [ ]
- [ ]
- [ ]
- [ ]
- [ ]
- [ ]
- [ ]
- [ ]
- [ ]
- [ ]
- [ ]

PHYSICAL NEEDS

EMOTIONAL NEEDS

HOW I FEEL TODAY

I WANT TO WORK ON...

Affirmations

DAILY AFFIRMATIONS

Yes, You Can!

IDEAS & PROMPTS

I'm in charge of how I feel today, and I'm choosing to be happy.

I'm brave enough to climb any mountain.

I have the power to change my story.

I've decided that I'm good enough.

No one can make me feel inferior.

My strength is greater than my struggle.

I'll use my failures as a stepping stone.

It's not their job to like me. It's mine.

Success will be my driving force.

The only person who can defeat me, is me.

I dare to be different.

I do not need other people to be happy.

I deserve love, happiness and success.

I am loved and I am wanted.

I will not apologize for being myself.

Positive Thinking

POSITIVE THOUGHTS:
WRITE DOWN YOUR FAVORITE INSPIRATIONAL PHRASE

Do what makes you Happy

AFFIRMATION:

Self Care Techniques

MIND

_____
_____
_____
_____
_____
_____
_____
_____
_____
_____
_____
_____

BODY

_____
_____
_____
_____
_____
_____
_____
_____
_____
_____
_____
_____

Good things take time

One Day at a Time

MONDAY'S MOOD

TUESDAY'S MOOD

WEDNESDAY'S MOOD

Good things take time

THURSDAY'S MOOD

One Day at a Time

FRIDAY'S MOOD

SATURDAY'S MOOD

SUNDAY'S MOOD

THOUGHTS & REFLECTIONS ABOUT THE PAST WEEK

Mood Meter

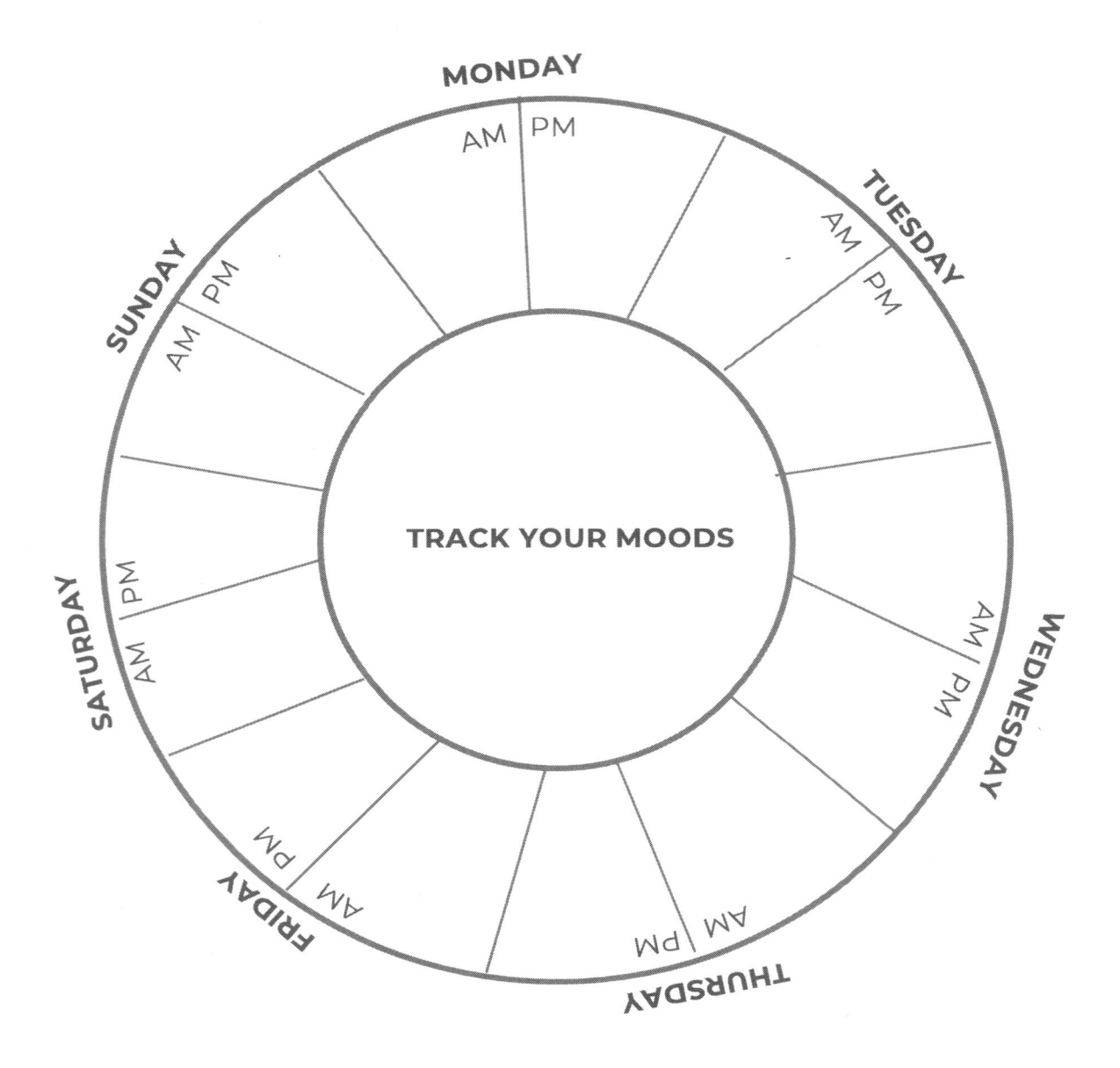

TRACK YOUR MOODS

- MONDAY — AM | PM
- TUESDAY — AM | PM
- WEDNESDAY — AM | PM
- THURSDAY — AM | PM
- FRIDAY — AM | PM
- SATURDAY — AM | PM
- SUNDAY — AM | PM

COLOR SCALE

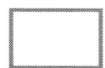

☐ 😄   ☐ 🙂   ☐ 🙁   ☐ 😟

Self Care Checklist

GOALS	M	T	W	T	F	S	S
Got enough rest	○	○	○	○	○	○	○
Spent time outdoors	○	○	○	○	○	○	○
Drank enough water	○	○	○	○	○	○	○
Spent time doing Something that makes me happy.	○	○	○	○	○	○	○
Went for a walk or exercised.	○	○	○	○	○	○	○
Spent time with family	○	○	○	○	○	○	○
Meditated	○	○	○	○	○	○	○
Connected with friends	○	○	○	○	○	○	○
_____	○	○	○	○	○	○	○
_____	○	○	○	○	○	○	○
_____	○	○	○	○	○	○	○

Me Time

Write down the things that make you happy. Then, check the box every day that you spend time with that activity.

Do what makes you Happy

Self Reflection

SELF REFLECTION: WHAT MAKES YOU HAPPY?

Each failure brings you one step closer to success

AFFIRMATION:

Grateful Thoughts

THIS WEEK I AM GRATEFUL FOR

I AM BLESSED TO HAVE THESE PEOPLE IN MY LIFE

5 REASONS TO BE THANKFUL

1
2
3
4
5

Self Care Log

HOW I CAN MINIMIZE THE NEGATIVITY IN MY LIFE

POSITIVE STEPS I CAN TAKE TO BE HAPPY

It Always Seems Impossible Until It's Done

DATE:

Positive Thinking

SELF CARE TO DO LIST:

- [ ] _____
- [ ] _____
- [ ] _____
- [ ] _____
- [ ] _____
- [ ] _____
- [ ] _____
- [ ] _____
- [ ] _____
- [ ] _____
- [ ] _____
- [ ] _____
- [ ] _____
- [ ] _____

PHYSICAL NEEDS

EMOTIONAL NEEDS

HOW I FEEL TODAY

I WANT TO WORK ON...

Affirmations

DAILY AFFIRMATIONS

IDEAS & PROMPTS

I'm in charge of how I feel today, and I'm choosing to be happy.

I'm brave enough to climb any mountain.

I have the power to change my story.

I've decided that I'm good enough.

No one can make me feel inferior.

My strength is greater than my struggle.

I'll use my failures as a stepping stone.

It's not their job to like me. It's mine.

Success will be my driving force.

The only person who can defeat me, is me.

I dare to be different.

I do not need other people to be happy.

I deserve love, happiness and success.

I am loved and I am wanted.

I will not apologize for being myself.

Yes, You Can!

Positive Thinking

POSITIVE THOUGHTS:
WRITE DOWN YOUR FAVORITE INSPIRATIONAL PHRASE

Do what makes you Happy

AFFIRMATION:

Self Care Techniques

MIND

_____
_____
_____
_____
_____
_____
_____
_____
_____
_____
_____

BODY

_____
_____
_____
_____
_____
_____
_____
_____
_____
_____
_____

Good things take time

One Day at a Time

MONDAY'S MOOD

TUESDAY'S MOOD

WEDNESDAY'S MOOD

Good things take time

THURSDAY'S MOOD

One Day at a Time

FRIDAY'S MOOD

SATURDAY'S MOOD

SUNDAY'S MOOD

THOUGHTS & REFLECTIONS ABOUT THE PAST WEEK

Mood Meter

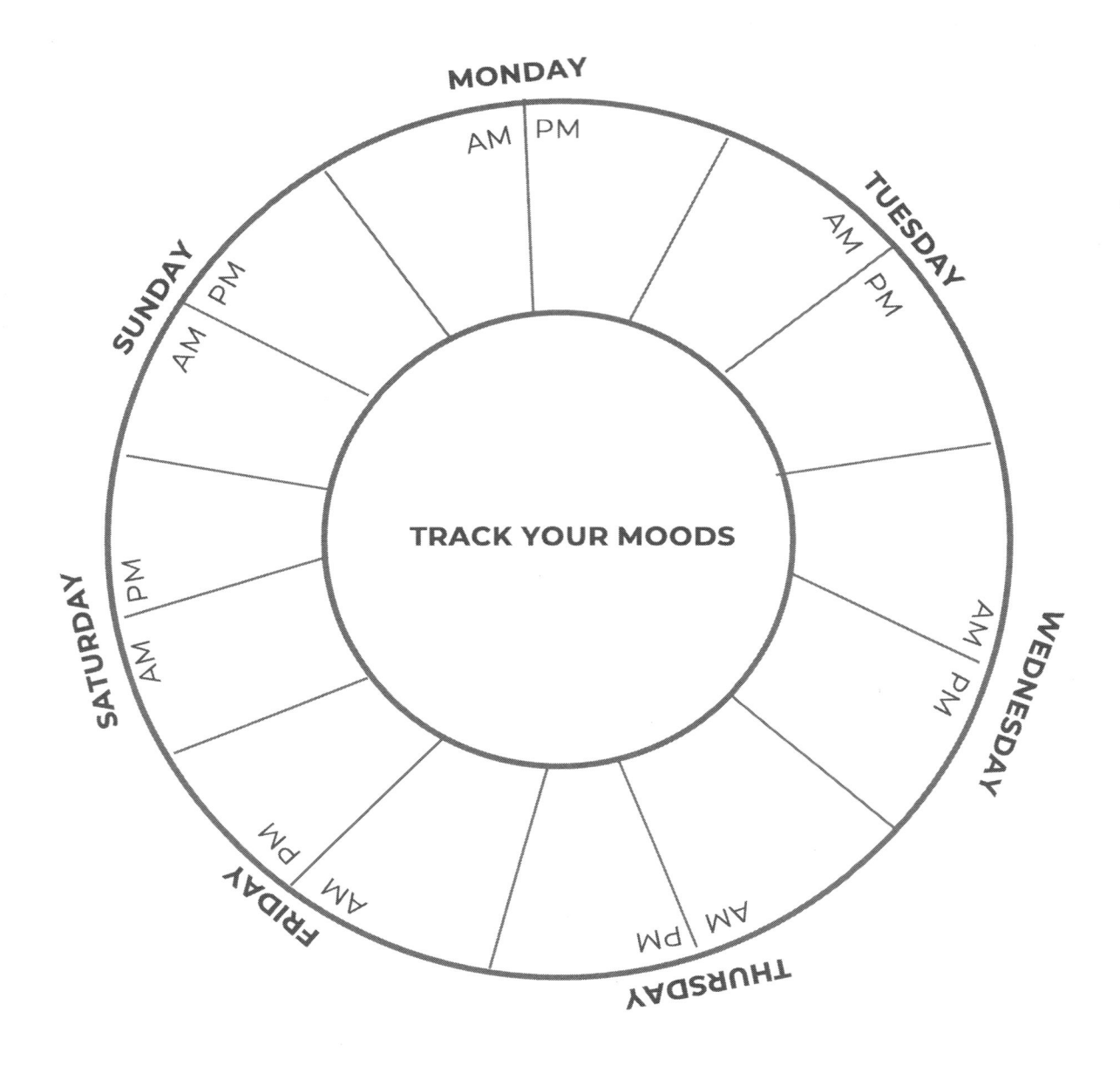

TRACK YOUR MOODS

- MONDAY AM | PM
- TUESDAY AM | PM
- WEDNESDAY AM | PM
- THURSDAY AM | PM
- FRIDAY AM | PM
- SATURDAY AM | PM
- SUNDAY AM | PM

COLOR SCALE

Self Care Checklist

GOALS	M	T	W	T	F	S	S
Got enough rest	○	○	○	○	○	○	○
Spent time outdoors	○	○	○	○	○	○	○
Drank enough water	○	○	○	○	○	○	○
Spent time doing Something that makes me happy.	○	○	○	○	○	○	○
Went for a walk or exercised.	○	○	○	○	○	○	○
Spent time with family	○	○	○	○	○	○	○
Meditated	○	○	○	○	○	○	○
Connected with friends	○	○	○	○	○	○	○
_____	○	○	○	○	○	○	○
_____	○	○	○	○	○	○	○
_____	○	○	○	○	○	○	○

Me Time

Write down the things that make you happy. Then, check the box every day that you spend time with that activity.

Do what makes you Happy

Self Reflection

SELF REFLECTION: WHAT MAKES YOU HAPPY?

Each failure brings you one step closer to success

AFFIRMATION:

Grateful Thoughts

THIS WEEK I AM GRATEFUL FOR

I AM BLESSED TO HAVE THESE PEOPLE IN MY LIFE

5 REASONS TO BE THANKFUL

1.
2.
3.
4.
5.

Self Care Log

HOW I CAN MINIMIZE THE NEGATIVITY IN MY LIFE

POSITIVE STEPS I CAN TAKE TO BE HAPPY

It Always Seems Impossible Until It's Done

DATE:

Positive Thinking

SELF CARE TO DO LIST:

- [ ] _____
- [ ] _____
- [ ] _____
- [ ] _____
- [ ] _____
- [ ] _____
- [ ] _____
- [ ] _____
- [ ] _____
- [ ] _____
- [ ] _____
- [ ] _____
- [ ] _____
- [ ] _____

PHYSICAL NEEDS

EMOTIONAL NEEDS

HOW I FEEL TODAY

I WANT TO WORK ON...

Affirmations

DAILY AFFIRMATIONS

Yes, You Can!

IDEAS & PROMPTS

I'm in charge of how I feel today, and I'm choosing to be happy.

I'm brave enough to climb any mountain.

I have the power to change my story.

I've decided that I'm good enough.

No one can make me feel inferior.

My strength is greater than my struggle.

I'll use my failures as a stepping stone.

It's not their job to like me. It's mine.

Success will be my driving force.

The only person who can defeat me, is me.

I dare to be different.

I do not need other people to be happy.

I deserve love, happiness and success.

I am loved and I am wanted.

I will not apologize for being myself.

Positive Thinking

POSITIVE THOUGHTS:
WRITE DOWN YOUR FAVORITE INSPIRATIONAL PHRASE

Do what makes you Happy

AFFIRMATION:

Self Care Techniques

MIND   **BODY**

Good things take time

One Day at a Time

MONDAY'S MOOD

TUESDAY'S MOOD

WEDNESDAY'S MOOD

Good things take time

THURSDAY'S MOOD

One Day at a Time

FRIDAY'S MOOD

SATURDAY'S MOOD

SUNDAY'S MOOD

THOUGHTS & REFLECTIONS ABOUT THE PAST WEEK

Mood Meter

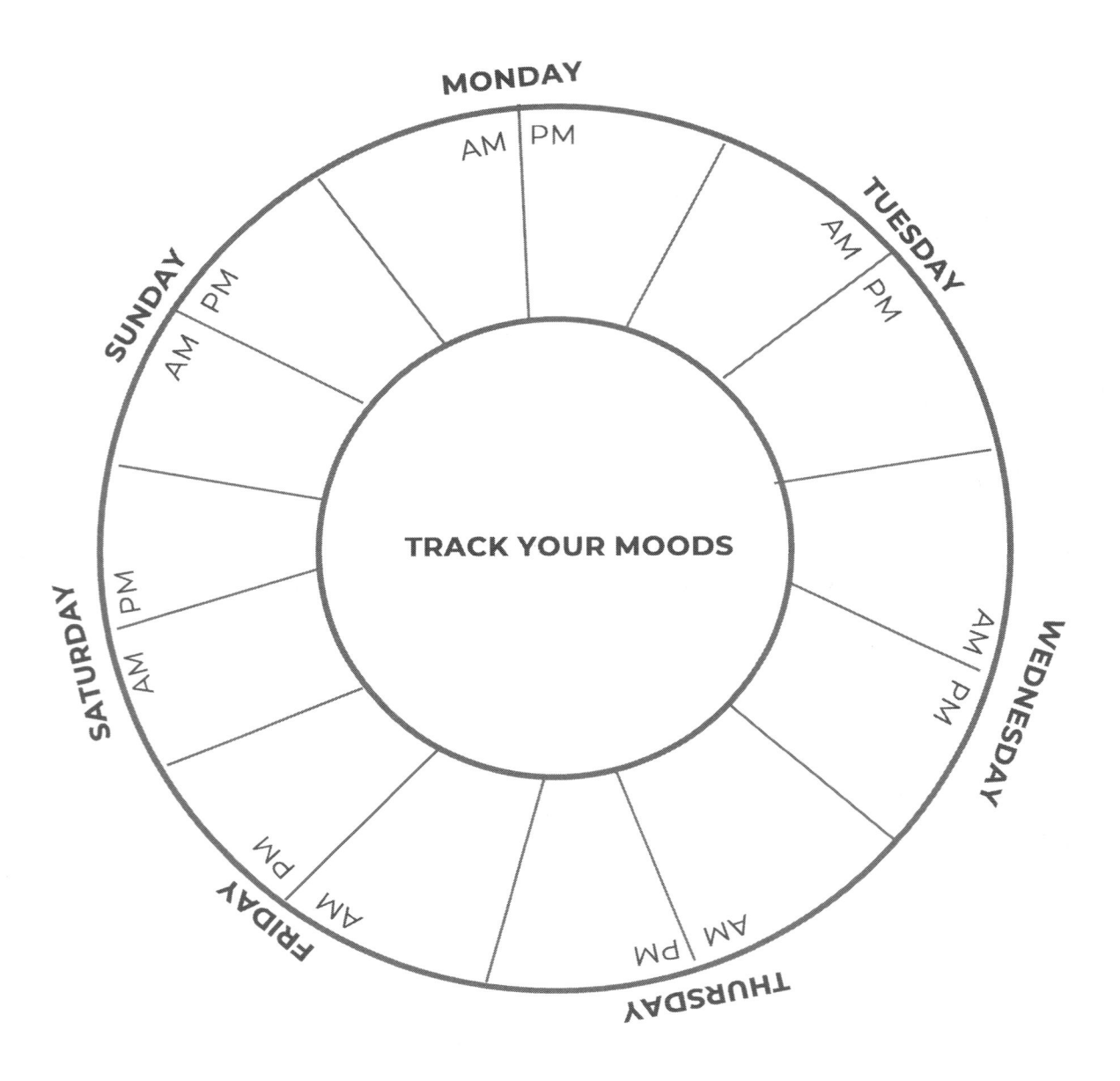

MONDAY | TUESDAY | WEDNESDAY | THURSDAY | FRIDAY | SATURDAY | SUNDAY
AM | PM

TRACK YOUR MOODS

COLOR SCALE

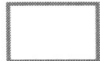

Self Care Checklist

GOALS	M	T	W	T	F	S	S
Got enough rest	○	○	○	○	○	○	○
Spent time outdoors	○	○	○	○	○	○	○
Drank enough water	○	○	○	○	○	○	○
Spent time doing Something that makes me happy.	○	○	○	○	○	○	○
Went for a walk or exercised.	○	○	○	○	○	○	○
Spent time with family	○	○	○	○	○	○	○
Meditated	○	○	○	○	○	○	○
Connected with friends	○	○	○	○	○	○	○
_____	○	○	○	○	○	○	○
_____	○	○	○	○	○	○	○
_____	○	○	○	○	○	○	○

Me Time

Write down the things that make you happy. Then, check the box every day that you spend time with that activity.

Do what makes you Happy

Self Reflection

SELF REFLECTION: WHAT MAKES YOU HAPPY?

Each failure brings you one step closer to success

AFFIRMATION:

Grateful Thoughts

THIS WEEK I AM GRATEFUL FOR

I AM BLESSED TO HAVE THESE PEOPLE IN MY LIFE

5 REASONS TO BE THANKFUL

1.
2.
3.
4.
5.

Self Care Log

HOW I CAN MINIMIZE THE NEGATIVITY IN MY LIFE

POSITIVE STEPS I CAN TAKE TO BE HAPPY

It Always Seems Impossible Until It's Done

DATE:

Positive Thinking

SELF CARE TO DO LIST:

- [ ] _____
- [ ] _____
- [ ] _____
- [ ] _____
- [ ] _____
- [ ] _____
- [ ] _____
- [ ] _____
- [ ] _____
- [ ] _____
- [ ] _____
- [ ] _____
- [ ] _____
- [ ] _____

PHYSICAL NEEDS

EMOTIONAL NEEDS

HOW I FEEL TODAY

I WANT TO WORK ON...

Affirmations

DAILY AFFIRMATIONS

IDEAS & PROMPTS

I'm in charge of how I feel today, and I'm choosing to be happy.

I'm brave enough to climb any mountain.

I have the power to change my story.

I've decided that I'm good enough.

No one can make me feel inferior.

My strength is greater than my struggle.

I'll use my failures as a stepping stone.

It's not their job to like me. It's mine.

Success will be my driving force.

The only person who can defeat me, is me.

I dare to be different.

I do not need other people to be happy.

I deserve love, happiness and success.

I am loved and I am wanted.

I will not apologize for being myself.

Yes, You Can!

Positive Thinking

POSITIVE THOUGHTS:
WRITE DOWN YOUR FAVORITE INSPIRATIONAL PHRASE

Do what makes you Happy

AFFIRMATION:

Self Care Techniques

MIND   **BODY**

Good things take time

One Day at a Time

MONDAY'S **MOOD**

TUESDAY'S **MOOD**

WEDNESDAY'S **MOOD**

Good things take time

THURSDAY'S **MOOD**

One Day at a Time

FRIDAY'S MOOD

SATURDAY'S MOOD

SUNDAY'S MOOD

THOUGHTS & REFLECTIONS ABOUT THE PAST WEEK

Mood Meter

MONDAY — AM | PM
TUESDAY — AM | PM
WEDNESDAY — AM | PM
THURSDAY — AM | PM
FRIDAY — AM | PM
SATURDAY — AM | PM
SUNDAY — AM | PM

TRACK YOUR MOODS

COLOR SCALE

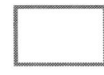

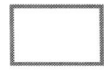

Self Care Checklist

GOALS	M	T	W	T	F	S	S
Got enough rest	○	○	○	○	○	○	○
Spent time outdoors	○	○	○	○	○	○	○
Drank enough water	○	○	○	○	○	○	○
Spent time doing Something that makes me happy.	○	○	○	○	○	○	○
Went for a walk or exercised.	○	○	○	○	○	○	○
Spent time with family	○	○	○	○	○	○	○
Meditated	○	○	○	○	○	○	○
Connected with friends	○	○	○	○	○	○	○
_____	○	○	○	○	○	○	○
_____	○	○	○	○	○	○	○
_____	○	○	○	○	○	○	○

Me Time

Write down the things that make you happy. Then, check the box every day that you spend time with that activity.

Do what makes you Happy

Self Reflection

SELF REFLECTION: WHAT MAKES YOU HAPPY?

Each failure brings you one step closer to success

AFFIRMATION:

Grateful Thoughts

THIS WEEK I AM GRATEFUL FOR

I AM BLESSED TO HAVE THESE PEOPLE IN MY LIFE

5 REASONS TO BE THANKFUL

1.
2.
3.
4.
5.

Self Care Log

HOW I CAN MINIMIZE THE NEGATIVITY IN MY LIFE

POSITIVE STEPS I CAN TAKE TO BE HAPPY

It Always Seems Impossible Until It's Done

DATE:

Positive Thinking

SELF CARE TO DO LIST:

- [ ] _____
- [ ] _____
- [ ] _____
- [ ] _____
- [ ] _____
- [ ] _____
- [ ] _____
- [ ] _____
- [ ] _____
- [ ] _____
- [ ] _____
- [ ] _____
- [ ] _____
- [ ] _____

PHYSICAL NEEDS

EMOTIONAL NEEDS

HOW I FEEL TODAY

I WANT TO WORK ON...

Affirmations

DAILY AFFIRMATIONS

Yes, You Can!

IDEAS & PROMPTS

I'm in charge of how I feel today, and I'm choosing to be happy.

I'm brave enough to climb any mountain.

I have the power to change my story.

I've decided that I'm good enough.

No one can make me feel inferior.

My strength is greater than my struggle.

I'll use my failures as a stepping stone.

It's not their job to like me. It's mine.

Success will be my driving force.

The only person who can defeat me, is me.

I dare to be different.

I do not need other people to be happy.

I deserve love, happiness and success.

I am loved and I am wanted.

I will not apologize for being myself.

Positive Thinking

POSITIVE THOUGHTS:
WRITE DOWN YOUR FAVORITE INSPIRATIONAL PHRASE

Do what makes you Happy

AFFIRMATION:

Self Care Techniques

MIND

_____
_____
_____
_____
_____
_____
_____
_____
_____
_____

BODY

_____
_____
_____
_____
_____
_____
_____
_____
_____
_____

Good things take time

One Day at a Time

MONDAY'S **MOOD**

TUESDAY'S **MOOD**

WEDNESDAY'S **MOOD**

Good things take time

THURSDAY'S **MOOD**

One Day at a Time

FRIDAY'S MOOD

SATURDAY'S MOOD

SUNDAY'S MOOD

THOUGHTS & REFLECTIONS ABOUT THE PAST WEEK

Mood Meter

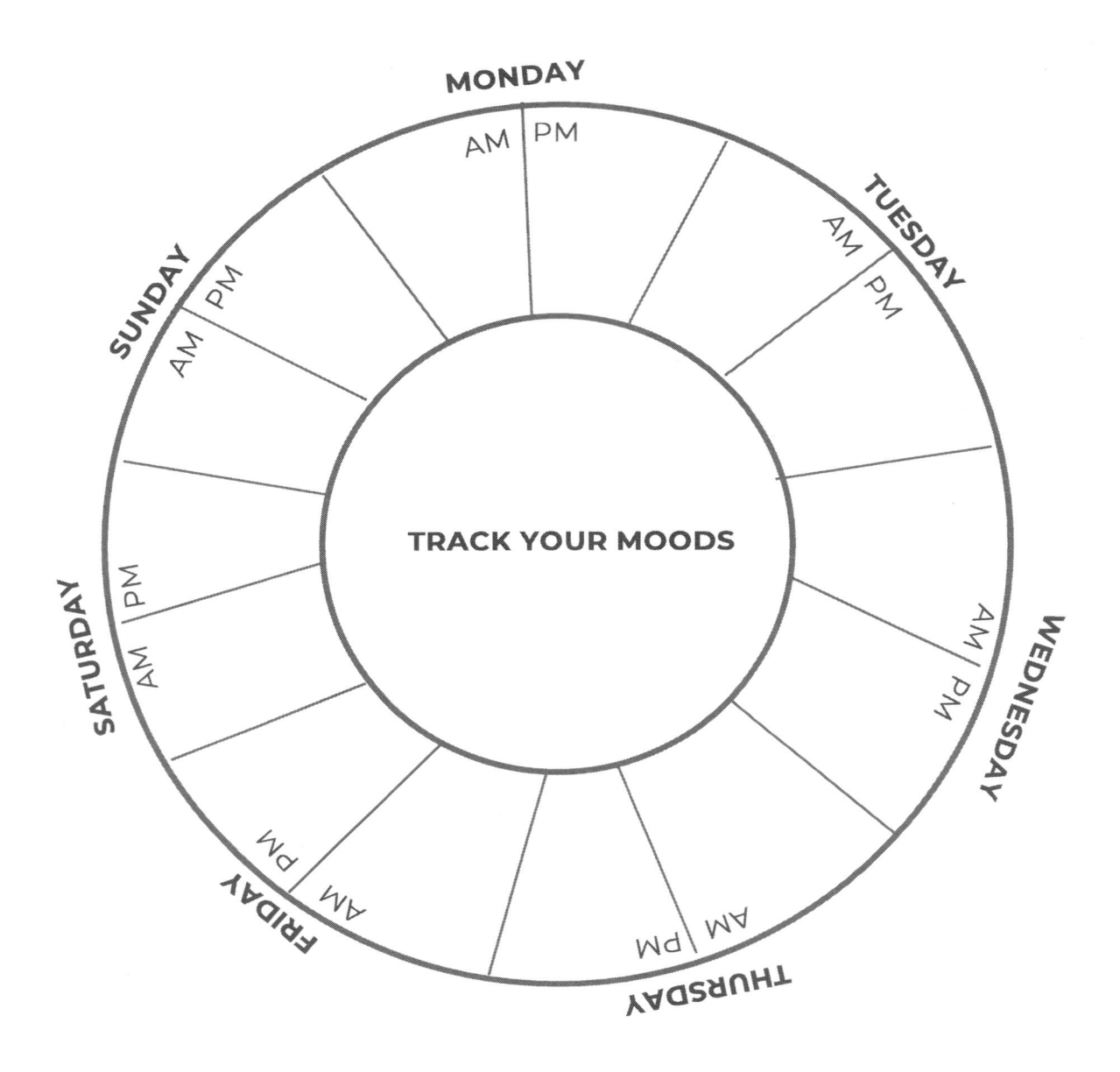

MONDAY — AM | PM
TUESDAY — AM | PM
WEDNESDAY — AM | PM
THURSDAY — AM | PM
FRIDAY — AM | PM
SATURDAY — AM | PM
SUNDAY — AM | PM

TRACK YOUR MOODS

COLOR SCALE

Self Care Checklist

GOALS	M	T	W	T	F	S	S
Got enough rest	○	○	○	○	○	○	○
Spent time outdoors	○	○	○	○	○	○	○
Drank enough water	○	○	○	○	○	○	○
Spent time doing Something that makes me happy.	○	○	○	○	○	○	○
Went for a walk or exercised.	○	○	○	○	○	○	○
Spent time with family	○	○	○	○	○	○	○
Meditated	○	○	○	○	○	○	○
Connected with friends	○	○	○	○	○	○	○
_____	○	○	○	○	○	○	○
_____	○	○	○	○	○	○	○
_____	○	○	○	○	○	○	○

Me Time

Write down the things that make you happy. Then, check the box every day that you spend time with that activity.

☆ Do what makes you Happy ☆

Self Reflection

SELF REFLECTION: WHAT MAKES YOU HAPPY?

Each failure brings you one step closer to success

AFFIRMATION:

Grateful Thoughts

THIS WEEK I AM GRATEFUL FOR

I AM BLESSED TO HAVE THESE PEOPLE IN MY LIFE

5 REASONS TO BE THANKFUL

1.
2.
3.
4.
5.

Self Care Log

HOW I CAN **MINIMIZE THE NEGATIVITY** IN MY LIFE

POSITIVE STEPS I CAN TAKE TO BE HAPPY

It Always Seems Impossible Until It's Done

DATE:

Positive Thinking

SELF CARE TO DO LIST:

- [ ] _____
- [ ] _____
- [ ] _____
- [ ] _____
- [ ] _____
- [ ] _____
- [ ] _____
- [ ] _____
- [ ] _____
- [ ] _____
- [ ] _____
- [ ] _____
- [ ] _____
- [ ] _____

PHYSICAL NEEDS

EMOTIONAL NEEDS

HOW I FEEL TODAY

I WANT TO WORK ON...

Affirmations

DAILY AFFIRMATIONS

IDEAS & PROMPTS

I'm in charge of how I feel today, and I'm choosing to be happy.

I'm brave enough to climb any mountain.

I have the power to change my story.

I've decided that I'm good enough.

No one can make me feel inferior.

My strength is greater than my struggle.

I'll use my failures as a stepping stone.

It's not their job to like me. It's mine.

Success will be my driving force.

The only person who can defeat me, is me.

I dare to be different.

I do not need other people to be happy.

I deserve love, happiness and success.

I am loved and I am wanted.

I will not apologize for being myself.

Yes, You Can!

Positive Thinking

POSITIVE THOUGHTS:
WRITE DOWN YOUR FAVORITE INSPIRATIONAL PHRASE

Do what makes you Happy

AFFIRMATION:

Self Care Techniques

MIND **BODY**

Good things take time

One Day at a Time

MONDAY'S MOOD

TUESDAY'S MOOD

WEDNESDAY'S MOOD

Good things take time

THURSDAY'S MOOD

One Day at a Time

FRIDAY'S MOOD

SATURDAY'S MOOD

SUNDAY'S MOOD

THOUGHTS & REFLECTIONS ABOUT THE PAST WEEK

Mood Meter

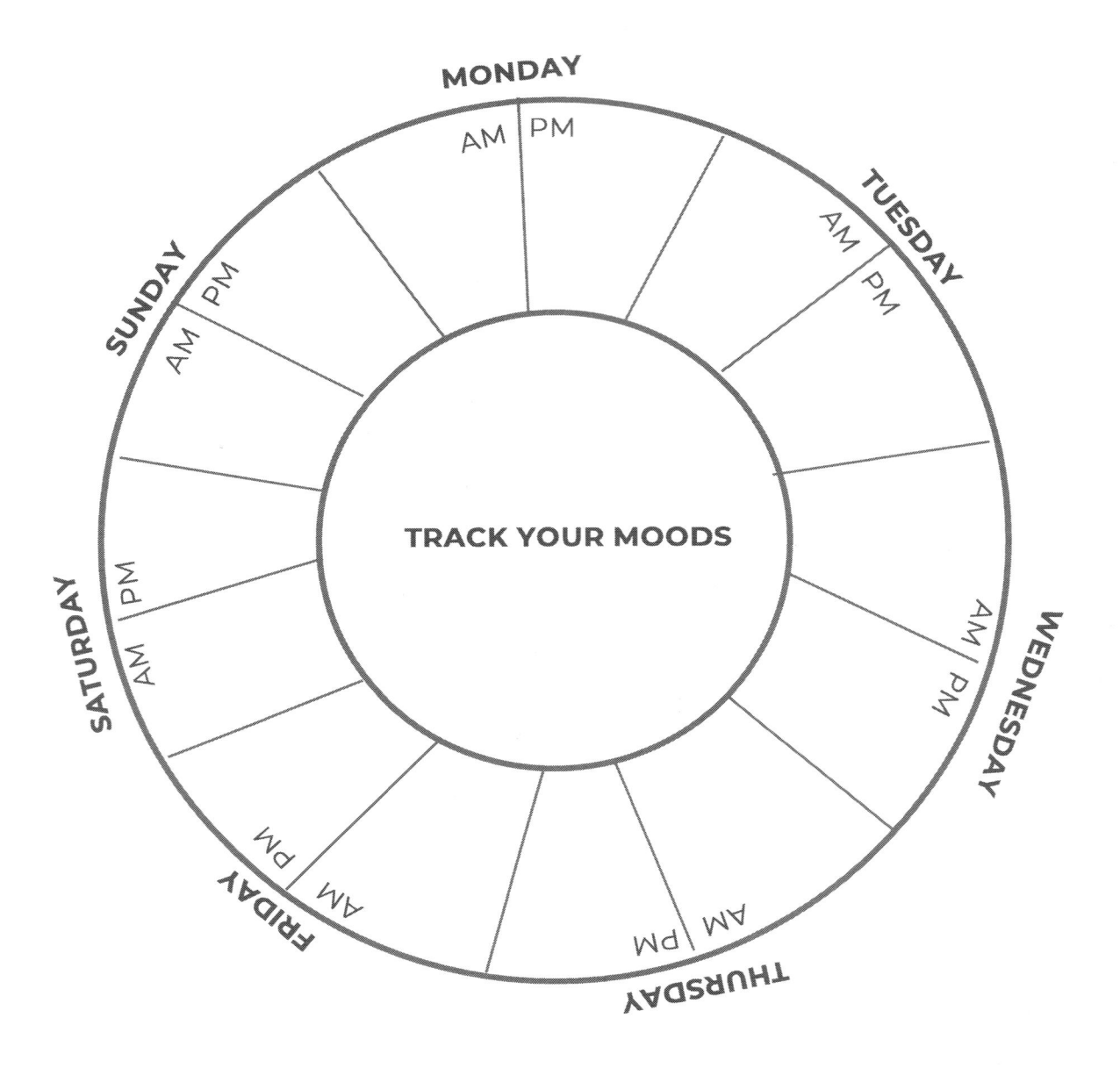

MONDAY
AM | PM

TUESDAY
AM | PM

WEDNESDAY
AM | PM

THURSDAY
AM | PM

FRIDAY
AM | PM

SATURDAY
AM | PM

SUNDAY
AM | PM

TRACK YOUR MOODS

COLOR SCALE

Self Care Checklist

GOALS	M	T	W	T	F	S	S
Got enough rest	○	○	○	○	○	○	○
Spent time outdoors	○	○	○	○	○	○	○
Drank enough water	○	○	○	○	○	○	○
Spent time doing Something that makes me happy.	○	○	○	○	○	○	○
Went for a walk or exercised.	○	○	○	○	○	○	○
Spent time with family	○	○	○	○	○	○	○
Meditated	○	○	○	○	○	○	○
Connected with friends	○	○	○	○	○	○	○
_____	○	○	○	○	○	○	○
_____	○	○	○	○	○	○	○
_____	○	○	○	○	○	○	○

Me Time

Write down the things that make you happy. Then, check the box every day that you spend time with that activity.

Do what makes you Happy

Self Reflection

SELF REFLECTION: WHAT MAKES YOU HAPPY?

Each failure brings you one step closer to success

AFFIRMATION:

Grateful Thoughts

THIS WEEK I AM GRATEFUL FOR

I AM BLESSED TO HAVE THESE PEOPLE IN MY LIFE

5 REASONS TO BE THANKFUL

1.
2.
3.
4.
5.

Self Care Log

HOW I CAN **MINIMIZE THE NEGATIVITY** IN MY LIFE

POSITIVE STEPS I CAN TAKE TO BE HAPPY

It Always Seems Impossible Until It's Done

DATE:

Positive Thinking

SELF CARE TO DO LIST:

- [ ] _____
- [ ] _____
- [ ] _____
- [ ] _____
- [ ] _____
- [ ] _____
- [ ] _____
- [ ] _____
- [ ] _____
- [ ] _____
- [ ] _____
- [ ] _____
- [ ] _____
- [ ] _____

PHYSICAL NEEDS

EMOTIONAL NEEDS

HOW I FEEL TODAY

I WANT TO WORK ON...

Affirmations

DAILY AFFIRMATIONS

Yes, You Can!

IDEAS & PROMPTS

I'm in charge of how I feel today, and I'm choosing to be happy.

I'm brave enough to climb any mountain.

I have the power to change my story.

I've decided that I'm good enough.

No one can make me feel inferior.

My strength is greater than my struggle.

I'll use my failures as a stepping stone.

It's not their job to like me. It's mine.

Success will be my driving force.

The only person who can defeat me, is me.

I dare to be different.

I do not need other people to be happy.

I deserve love, happiness and success.

I am loved and I am wanted.

I will not apologize for being myself.

Positive Thinking

POSITIVE THOUGHTS:
WRITE DOWN YOUR FAVORITE INSPIRATIONAL PHRASE

Do what makes you Happy

AFFIRMATION:

Self Care Techniques

MIND

BODY

Good things take time

One Day at a Time

MONDAY'S MOOD

TUESDAY'S MOOD

WEDNESDAY'S MOOD

Good things take time

THURSDAY'S MOOD

One Day at a Time

FRIDAY'S MOOD

SATURDAY'S MOOD

SUNDAY'S MOOD

THOUGHTS & REFLECTIONS ABOUT THE PAST WEEK

Mood Meter

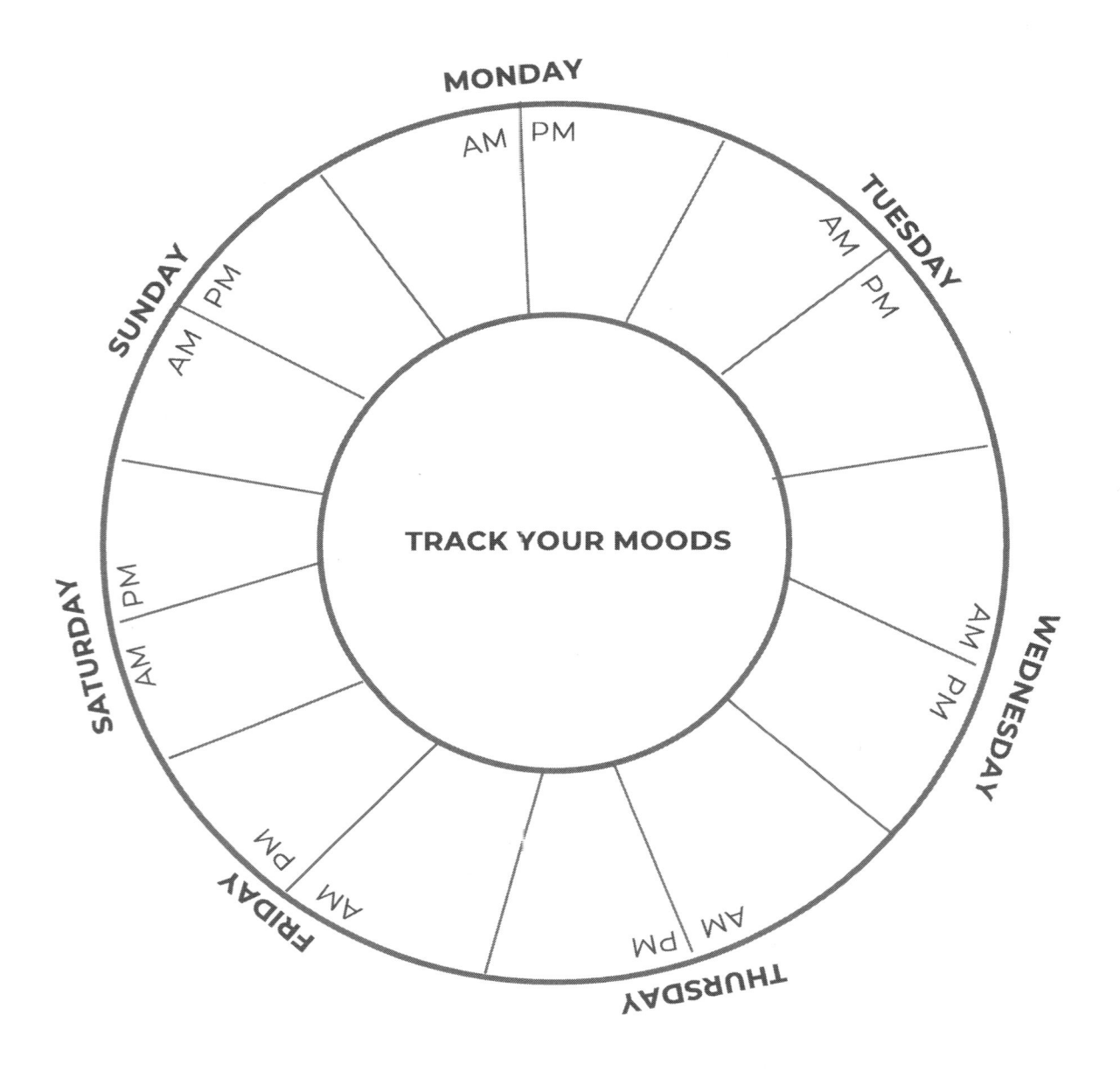

TRACK YOUR MOODS

- MONDAY AM | PM
- TUESDAY AM | PM
- WEDNESDAY AM | PM
- THURSDAY AM | PM
- FRIDAY AM | PM
- SATURDAY AM | PM
- SUNDAY AM | PM

COLOR SCALE

Self Care Checklist

GOALS   M   T   W   T   F   S   S

- Got enough rest
- Spent time outdoors
- Drank enough water
- Spent time doing Something that makes me happy.
- Went for a walk or exercised.
- Spent time with family
- Meditated
- Connected with friends
- _____
- _____
- _____

Me Time

Write down the things that make you happy. Then, check the box every day that you spend time with that activity.

Do what makes you Happy

Self Reflection

SELF REFLECTION: WHAT MAKES YOU HAPPY?

Each failure brings you one step closer to success

AFFIRMATION:

Grateful Thoughts

THIS WEEK I AM GRATEFUL FOR

I AM BLESSED TO HAVE THESE PEOPLE IN MY LIFE

5 REASONS TO BE THANKFUL

1.
2.
3.
4.
5.

Self Care Log

HOW I CAN MINIMIZE THE NEGATIVITY IN MY LIFE

POSITIVE STEPS I CAN TAKE TO BE HAPPY

It Always Seems Impossible Until It's Done

DATE:

Made in the USA
Columbia, SC
03 December 2024